FINANCIAL FEMINIST MANUAL

A modern woman's guide on how to develop financial mastery, control her money and create a life she loves.

By

Crista C. Kauffman

TABLE OF CONTENTS

INTRODUCTION

Feminism is a powerful movement that stands up for fairness between all genders. Its mission is to tackle things that might not be quite right in how people are treated. This includes looking closely at how society, politics, and jobs treat different folks. But hold on, here's a cool twist! There's this fantastic idea known as "financial feminism," where the incredible principles of feminism join forces with a mission to make money matters fair and equal, especially for women.

So, think of a financial feminist as a superhero for money matters. This superhero isn't content with sitting around; they're all about taking action and using their voice. They're like champions who want to ensure that women can be strong, independent money managers and get the same chances as anyone else.

Being a financial feminist is a bit like putting on a cape and stepping out to make a positive impact. It involves things like supporting rules that guarantee everyone gets paid fairly, no matter their gender, when they do the same work. It's cheering for women to step up and take charge in places where money decisions are made, like big banks. It's also giving a big thumbs-up to making sure women know all the savvy money moves so they can truly master their finances.

In a nutshell, a financial feminist strives to even the playing field. They're determined to tackle the money-related gaps and obstacles that women might come across. Their goal is to craft a financial world that's fairer and more inclusive, where everyone can thrive and succeed, no matter their gender.

When we talk about being money-wise, we're talking about understanding all sorts of money stuff – like how budgets work, why saving is important, and how to make smart choices with your hard-earned cash.

It's like having a special toolbox for making really smart decisions about your money. Research has proven that having this toolbox, which we call financial literacy, is a big deal. It can make a huge difference in how good you feel about money in the long run.

Now, let's delve into the correlation between financial intelligence and women. There are numerous captivating things waiting to be discovered.

CHAPTER ONE

KEY THINGS TO NOTE ABOUT FINANCIAL LITERACY

- **Knowledge is Key:** Imagine financial literacy as a treasure trove of knowledge. With this treasure, women can confidently steer their financial ships. They're like captains who know how to navigate the money seas.

- **A Shield of Security:** Financial literacy acts like a shield against unexpected financial storms. It prepares women for life's twists and turns, ensuring they're not caught off guard when money gets tricky.

- **Boosting Empowerment:** When women are financially literate, they feel empowered and in control. It's like having a key to open doors of opportunity and freedom.

- **Striving for Equality:** Financial literacy can help level the playing field between men and women in the financial realm. It's like giving women the tools they need to stand equally with men when dealing with money.

- **Breaking Barriers:** In many places, women have faced barriers in learning about money. But with financial literacy, these barriers start to crumble. It's like opening up a world full of possibilities and choices.

- **Laying Strong Foundations:** Just as a solid foundation is crucial for a sturdy building, financial literacy lays the groundwork for a secure financial future. When women have this foundation, they're better equipped to tackle challenges and build a bright financial future.

So, when you put all these puzzle pieces together, you realize that financial literacy isn't just about numbers and budgets. It's about giving women the tools, knowledge, and confidence to take control of their financial destinies, make smart decisions, and pave the way for a future where everyone is on equal ground.

Gender Disparity in Financial Literacy

Studies have consistently shown that when it comes to understanding money matters, there's a gap between men and women. Generally, women tend to score lower on tests that measure financial knowledge compared to their male counterparts. This difference in scores can be explained by a variety of reasons, including social expectations, cultural traditions, differences in education opportunities, and how easy it is for each gender to access information about handling money.

Let's dive a bit deeper into what's going on:

- **Social and Cultural Influences:** Sometimes, the way we're raised and the roles society expects us to play can affect how we learn about money. For instance, if a culture or community emphasizes that women should focus on certain responsibilities and men on others, it might impact how much they learn about finances.

- **Education Opportunities:** Education is like a key that

unlocks doors of knowledge. If there are differences in the education opportunities provided to boys and girls, it can lead to variations in financial literacy. Imagine if boys are encouraged to take more math or business classes, while girls are directed towards different subjects. This could affect how comfortable each gender feels with money topics.

- **Access to Financial Info:** Picture this – if you want to learn something new, you need the right tools and resources. When it comes to learning about money, having access to information like books, websites, and workshops is important. If one gender has an easier time accessing these resources, it could give them an advantage in becoming financially literate.

- **Breaking Stereotypes:** Sometimes, we're held back by stereotypes. If people believe that managing money is more of a "guy thing," it might discourage girls from learning about it. Overcoming these stereotypes is crucial to bridging the gender gap in financial knowledge.

- **Confidence Matters:** Imagine trying to learn something when you're not sure if you're "supposed" to know it. That can affect your confidence in tackling the subject. Women might face this kind of challenge in the world of finance, which could impact their willingness to engage and learn. It's important to understand that this gender gap isn't because one gender is naturally better with money. It's about the different opportunities and environments each gender faces. The good news is that we can work towards closing this gap by providing equal education and resources to everyone, breaking down stereotypes, and encouraging both men and women to feel confident and capable when it comes to handling their finances.

- **Socioeconomic Factors and Money Smarts:** Where you come from and how much money you have can affect how well you understand finances. For instance, women in families with less money or those who haven't had many opportunities might not get to learn much about money, and that can make it harder for them to be good with money.

Remember, the connection between where you come from and how well you know about money is a big deal. If you don't have the chance to learn about money and how it all works, it's like trying to play a game without knowing the rules. And that can make things pretty challenging, especially when it comes to making decisions about money.

Women's Changing Role in Finance

The part that women play in finance has changed a lot over time, and they've done some really good things in an area that used to be mostly for men. Even though things have gotten better, there are still things that need to be fixed. Here are some important points about how women are involved in finance;

- **Representation:**

In the past, there weren't many women in finance, especially in the higher-up jobs. But now, people are trying to make things fairer by having more women in the finance world. More women are choosing to work in finance these days.

- **Financial Jobs:**

Women work in different jobs in finance, like looking at numbers, being accountants, helping with investments, giving financial advice, managing funds, understanding the economy, and more.

- **Leading and Managing:**

Even though there are still fewer women in the top boss positions, more women are becoming bosses and managers in finance. People are starting to pay attention to having women in charge.

- **Getting Paid Fairly:**

Just like in other jobs, sometimes women get paid less than men in finance. But people are trying to fix this and make sure that women get the same pay for the same work.

- **Financial Education:**

Women are learning more about how money works and how to make good money choices. This helps them feel strong and able to make smart decisions about their money.

- **Advocacy and Networks:**

There are groups and places where women in finance can get help and make friends. These groups offer advice, chances to meet new people, and useful things for women's careers.

- **Entrepreneurship:**
Women are also starting their own money-related businesses or new tech ideas in finance, which is pretty cool.

- **Impact Investing:**
Women are also making changes in how they use their money. They're investing in things that help the world and make it better, not just for money but also for good things, for people and the planet.

- **Balancing Work and Life:**
Just like in other jobs, women in finance might have some trouble balancing their jobs with their lives,

especially if they also take care of family members.

In the end, women's role in finance is still changing, and people are working hard to make things more equal and fairer. Even though things have improved, there's still stuff to do to make sure women get the same chances and are seen in all parts of finance.

CHAPTER TWO

THE FEELINGS ABOUT MONEY

Money, which seems like a regular part of modern life, can make people feel all sorts of things. It can bring happiness and safety, but also worry and wanting more. How we feel about money affects what we think, what we do, and the choices we make.

Money's Mixed Feelings

Money is supposed to help us trade things and decide how much stuff is worth. But it has come to mean much more. On one side, money can make us feel like we have freedom. It gives us chances to grow, be financially stable, and go after our dreams. When we achieve our goals, it can make us feel happy, content, and proud.

On the flip side, money can also make us feel stressed and upset. When there isn't enough money, or when we see others having more, it can make us feel anxious, jealous, and not good enough. Trying too hard to get a lot of money can even make us forget about important things like friends and feeling good, which can leave us feeling empty even if we have lots of things.

What Others Think and Society

Our feelings about money also come from what our family and the people around us say. Our culture, where we come from, and what society thinks also shape how we see money. Some places make us think being rich is amazing, while others say being kind and peaceful is more important.

Furthermore, the media and advertising industry make us believe that happiness and contentment are attainable through material possessions and luxury. Seeing these messages a lot can make us feel bad if we can't get all the cool things we see. We might start to feel like we're not enough if we don't have as much as others.

How Money Makes Us Feel

Getting a lot of money can change how we feel. At first, we might feel proud and strong, but then we might worry we'll lose it all. People with a lot of money can even feel guilty, like they're doing something wrong. And people who don't have much money can feel frustrated and powerless.

Can Money Buy Happiness?

Some think money can make us happy. Indeed, having enough money for things like food and a place to live can make us happier. But the more money we get, the less it adds to our happiness. It's like when we get used to something and it doesn't make us as happy anymore.

And always comparing ourselves to people with more money can make us feel like we're not good enough. This keeps us wanting more money, even if it doesn't really make us happier.

Our feelings about money are a mix of what we believe, what people around us think, and how we see ourselves. Money can make us feel good and bad, but it's just one part of life. It's important to find a balance between money goals and feeling good. Remember, money can't buy everything, and being happy is about more than just having lots of money.

Relationship with money and understanding its limitations, Women can approach wealth with a more balanced and emotionally resilient mindset.

CHAPTER THREE

HOW TO HANDLE YOUR MONEY BETTER

Being good with money is important. It helps you feel safe about your finances and makes life less stressful.

Here's how you can make sure you're handling your money well:

- **Make a Plan for Your Money**

First, figure out how much money you make and spend each month. Split your spending into things you need, like bills, and things you want, like treats. Stick to your plan and change it when you need to.

- **Keep Track of Your Spending**

Write down everything you spend money on. Some apps and spreadsheets can help you see where your money goes. This helps you see if there are places where you can spend less.

- **Have Money for Emergencies**

It's a good idea to have some money saved up. Aim for having enough to cover your living expenses for three to six months. This is like a safety net for unexpected money troubles.

- **Be Smart About Debt**

If you owe money, start with paying off the debts that have the highest interest rates, like credit card debt. Paying more than the minimum amount helps you save on interest.

- **Save and Invest**

Set aside a part of your income to save. Besides your emergency fund, save money for big things like a house or for when you stop working. Think about investing some money in stocks, bonds, or retirement accounts to make your money grow.

- **Live Within Your Means**

Don't spend more than you earn. When you make more money, don't rush to spend it all. Instead, save and invest it to make your future better.

- **Think Before You Buy**

Before you buy something expensive, think if it's worth it and if it fits your money goals.

- **Exercise Discipline**

Practice self-control and don't make quick decisions about money. Stay focused on your long-term goals.

- **Pay Your Bills on Time**

Pay your bills when they're due to avoid extra fees.

- **Review and Adjust**

Look at your budget, savings, and investments regularly. Make changes if needed to stay on track.

- **Seek Professional Advice**

If you're uncertain about managing your finances, consider consulting a financial advisor for personalized guidance.

Practical Steps for Financial Control

Managing your spending and keeping a close watch on your expenses is a critical aspect of maintaining a stable financial situation and achieving your long-term financial goals. Here are some actionable strategies to help you take control of your spending:

- **Creating a Budget:**

Start by creating a detailed budget that outlines both your monthly income and expenses. Categorize your spending into different groups such as essential needs (like housing, utilities, and groceries), debt payments, savings, and discretionary spending (like entertainment, dining out, and shopping). A budget gives you a clear picture of your financial situation and helps you identify areas where you can cut back.

- **Keeping Track of Your Expenses:**

Record every expense, no matter how small. You can use budgeting apps, spreadsheets, or a simple notebook to track your daily spending. This practice raises your awareness of your spending patterns and helps you identify places where you might be spending too much.

- **Setting Financial Goals:**

Establish clear financial goals that match your priorities. Whether it's saving for a home down payment, paying off debts, or building an emergency fund, having specific goals motivates you to control your spending and allocate more funds toward achieving these objectives.

- **Distinguishing Between Needs and Wants:**

Before making a purchase, question whether it's something you truly need or just something you want. Be honest with yourself about whether the expense is crucial for your well-being and financial security.

- **Practicing the 24-Hour Rule:** For non-urgent purchases, follow the 24-hour rule. Delay the purchase for a day or two. This gives you time to think and decide if the expense is worthwhile or if it's simply a spontaneous decision.

- **Avoiding Impulse Spending:** Steer clear of making unplanned purchases. Instead, make a shopping list and stick to it when you go shopping, whether in stores or online. This reduces the likelihood of making impulsive buys.

- **Opting for Cash or Debit Cards:** Use cash or a debit card for discretionary spending instead of credit cards. Physically seeing the money leave your wallet makes you more aware of your spending choices.

- **Limiting Online Shopping:** Online shopping makes it easy to overspend with just a few clicks. Be mindful of your online shopping habits and consider limiting your access to shopping sites or removing stored credit card information to prevent impulsive buying.

- **Embracing Frugality:** Search for opportunities to save money in your daily life, such as using coupons, shopping during sales, buying in bulk, or choosing generic brands over pricier ones.

- **Avoiding Emotional Spending:** Emotional spending can lead to impulsive purchases. Find healthier ways to cope with stress or negative emotions, such as engaging in physical activities, pursuing hobbies, or spending quality time with loved ones.

- **Being Accountable:** Share your financial goals with a trusted friend or family member who can provide support and keep you on track with responsible spending.

- **Celebrating Small Achievements:** Acknowledge and celebrate your progress in managing your spending and reaching financial milestones. Positive reinforcement strengthens your commitment to good financial habits.

CHAPTER FOUR

CRAFTING YOUR MONEY MANAGEMENT PLAN

A money management plan, often referred to as a budgetary game plan, is a structured strategy for handling your finances. Its purpose is to guide you in achieving your financial aspirations, building wealth, and maintaining a stable financial standing. An intelligently designed money management plan can support you in budgeting effectively, saving prudently, investing wisely, and alleviating debt.

A well-defined budgetary strategy is essential for prudent financial management. It provides a roadmap for decision-making, helps to avoid overspending, promotes financial stability, and allows for progress towards financial goals.

Let's delve into a step-by-step guide to creating a fundamental money management plan:

Step 1: Evaluate Your Financial Situation

Commence by gaining a comprehensive understanding of your current financial position. Compile information about your earnings, expenditures, debts, assets, and liabilities. Create a comprehensive list of all your financial accounts along with their respective balances.

Step 2: Set Financial Objectives

Define your financial objectives spanning short-term, medium-term, and long-term timeframes. These objectives may encompass establishing an emergency fund, saving for a home's down payment, eliminating debt, or preparing for retirement.

Step 3: Construct a Budget

A budget serves as the cornerstone of your money management plan. Monitor your income and expenses to fathom where your funds are being allocated. Categorize your expenses into essential needs (e.g., housing, utilities, groceries) and discretionary indulgences (e.g., entertainment, dining out). It's imperative that your income exceeds your expenses, with a designated portion dedicated to savings and investments.

Step 4: Cultivate an Emergency Fund

Allocate a certain sum into an accessible account, such as a savings account, designated for unforeseen expenses or emergencies. Endeavor to accumulate an emergency fund equivalent to three to six months' worth of living expenditures.

Step 5: Curtail Debt

Should you carry high-interest debts like credit card debt, prioritize their settlement with vigor. Explore approaches such as the debt snowball method (clearing the smallest debt first) or the debt avalanche method (paying off the highest interest debt first).

Step 6: Allocate Funds for Savings and Investments

Direct a segment of your earnings towards long-term savings and investments. Contemplate contributing to retirement accounts. Employ diversification strategies to diffuse risk across your investment portfolio.

Step 7: Review and Fine-Tune

Periodically reassess your money management plan and gauge your progress toward achieving your financial objectives. Adjust the plan as necessary to account for alterations in income, expenses, or financial goals.

Step 8: Steer Clear of Impulsive Spending

Practice mindfulness regarding your spending habits and abstain from impromptu purchases. Before committing to a significant expenditure, scrutinize whether it aligns with your financial ambitions.

Step 9: Expand Your Financial Knowledge

Engage in a continual journey of learning about personal finance, investment strategies, and effective money management. Enhanced comprehension translates to more informed decision-making.

Step 10: Seek Expert Guidance

If navigating your financial matters leaves you uncertain or if you confront intricate financial scenarios, contemplate enlisting the services of a financial advisor. Their expertise can aid in creating a customized money management plan tailored to your unique circumstances.

Remember, the key to successful money management is discipline, consistency, and a long-term perspective. By implementing a well-thought-out money management plan, you can work towards achieving your financial objectives and secure a more stable and prosperous financial future.

CHAPTER FIVE

BECOMING DEBT-FREE

Embarking on the journey to become debt-free is a substantial financial goal that can grant you a profound sense of autonomy and security. This transformative quest involves extinguishing all outstanding debts, whether they be credit card balances, personal loans, student loans, or mortgages. While the path to debt freedom calls for unwavering resolve and diligent efforts, it is well within your reach with careful strategizing and steadfast dedication. Here's a roadmap to guide you on your expedition towards debt-free living:

- **Evaluate Your Debts**

Commence by amassing all pertinent debt details; balances, interest rates, and minimum monthly payments. This comprehensive assessment will unveil the complete panorama of your debt obligation.

- **Construct a Comprehensive Budget**

Forge a meticulously structured budget to monitor your income and outlays. Channel the bulk of your disposable income towards debt repayment while adequately addressing essential living expenditures.

- **Prioritize Debt Repayment**

Compile your debts in an ordered hierarchy. opt for a strategy that resonates with you: extinguishing high-interest debts first (debt avalanche method) or eliminating smaller debts initially (debt snowball method) for a motivational boost.

- **Prune Unnecessary Expenditures**

Identify spheres where discretionary spending can be curtailed. Rethink non-essential outlays to liberate additional funds earmarked for debt settlement.

- **Enhance Your Earnings**

Deliberate on diversifying your income streams—part-time engagements, freelance work, or selling surplus items. This supplementary income can expedite your debt-repayment endeavors.

- **Negotiate with Creditors**

Should meeting payment obligations become arduous, initiate discussions with your creditors. Explore potential options, such as diminished interest rates or revised payment schemes. Some creditors may exhibit a willingness to collaborate for manageable debt resolution.

- **Forge an Emergency Fund**

While debt obliteration remains paramount, safeguard a modest emergency fund to counter unforeseen expenses. This safeguards you from resorting to credit cards during exigencies.

- **Sustain Motivation**

The journey to debt freedom can be protracted; thus, nurturing your motivation is crucial. Celebrate each debt milestone and remind yourself of the manifold perks of debt-free living.

- **Shun Fresh Debt**

While on your debt-repudiation odyssey, resist the allure of accruing new debt. Scrutinize your spending habits, assessing whether purchases are indispensable before their execution.

- **Ponder Debt Consolidation**

If ensnared by numerous high-interest debts, mulling over debt consolidation may prove advantageous. This entails amalgamating debts into a lower-interest loan or balance transfer credit card, potentially curbing interest and streamlining debt management.

- **Seek Proficient Counsel**

Should the burden of debt appear insurmountable or devising a repayment plan seem intricate, contemplate enlisting assistance from a financial advisor or a respected credit counseling agency.

CHAPTER SIX

EMBARKING ON YOUR INVESTMENT JOURNEY

Investing is a key part of managing your money and building wealth. It involves putting money into things like businesses or projects to make a profit or achieve long-term financial goals. It's an important way to improve your finances and work toward your dreams. There are different types of investments, each with its risks and chances to make more money. Every investment harbors an element of risk, and assurances of profits remain elusive. Striking a balance between risk and reward, one that echoes your financial objectives and comfort threshold stands paramount.

Launching an investment career can be an exciting and rewarding journey, but it requires careful planning, education, and a commitment to continuous learning. Here are some steps to help you get started on your investment career:

- **Acquire Profound Knowledge**

Embark by immersing yourself in the rudiments of investment. Imbibe knowledge from books, articles, and online courses spanning investing, finance, and economics. Familiarize yourself with diverse investment avenues, spanning stocks, bonds, mutual funds, real estate, and alternative investments.

- **Set Forth Clear Objectives**

Deliberate and elucidate your investment aspirations and your affinity for risk. Ascertain whether your pursuit entails long-term expansion, income generation, or a fusion of both. Your objectives will steer the course of your investment strategy.

- **Construct a Sturdy Financial Foundation**

Before leaping into investments, lay a robust financial groundwork. Discharge high-interest debt, establish an emergency fund, and validate the extent of your insurance coverage

- **Embark with Modesty**

Commence your journey with investments harmonizing with your risk threshold and financial goals. Ponder low-cost index funds or exchange-traded funds (ETFs) as an unassuming approach to procure diversified market exposure.

- **Open Investment Accounts**

Depending on your country and location, open investment accounts like brokerage accounts, retirement accounts or tax-efficient accounts.

- **Diversify Your Portfolio**

Allocate your investments across different types of assets and industries to minimize risk. Employing diversification safeguards your portfolio from being heavily influenced by the performance of a single investment

- **Remain Well-Informed**

Stay abreast of financial news and market trends. Monitor your investments regularly, and base decisions on sound data and discerning analysis.

- **Sculpt an Investment Strategy**

Mold an investment strategy guided by your objectives, risk threshold, and temporal horizon. Reflect on whether you'll adopt an active investor stance or opt for a more passive, buy-and-hold demeanor.

- **Seek Counsel from Professionals**

In moments of uncertainty, contemplate soliciting guidance from a financial advisor. A seasoned professional can help you delineate a personalized investment blueprint and extend invaluable insights.

- **Cultivate Patience and Tenacity**

Investment is a protracted voyage. Shun impulsive choices spurred by short-term market undulations. Stick resolutely to your strategy and exude steadfastness in your approach.

- **Network and learn from others**

Partaking in dialogues with fellow investors and investment experts through virtual forums, investment collectives, or networking symposiums. Gleaning wisdom from seasoned investors can prove immensely enlightening.

- **Persist in the Pursuit of Knowledge**

The landscape of investment is in perpetual flux. Persevere in cultivating your inquisitiveness, consistently broadening your insight concerning fresh investment vistas, financial instruments, and market drifts.

Bear in mind that investing involves risk, and there are no guarantees of returns. Be prepared for the possibility of losses and be patient with your investments. As your career progresses, your knowledge and experience will grow, allowing you to refine your investment approach and make more informed decisions.

Common investment options

- **Stocks**

Stocks epitomize ownership in companies. Acquiring shares,

metamorphoses you into a shareholder, and your investment's worth oscillates in tandem with the company's performance and market dynamics.

- **Bonds**

Bonds, akin to debt securities, emanate from governments or corporations. Procuring a bond equates to extending a loan to the issuer, entitling you to interest disbursements and principal reimbursement upon the bond's maturation.

- **Mutual Funds**

Mutual funds amalgamate capital from multiple investors to fund an assorted portfolio of stocks, bonds, or other assets. These funds are shepherded by adept fund managers.

- **Exchange-traded funds (ETFs)**

ETFs mirror mutual funds but trade on stock exchanges akin to individual stocks. These vehicles bestow diversification and liquidity.

- **Real Estate**

Investing in real estate entails procuring properties for rental income or capital augmentation. The ambit spans residential and commercial properties.

- **Commodities**

Commodities encompass tangible goods such as gold, silver, oil, agricultural produce, and more.

Investors may engage in commodities trading via futures contracts or funnel investments into commodity-focused funds.

- **Certificates of Deposit (CDs)**

CDs represent fixed-rate time deposits extended by banks. They offer a modicum of risk but proffer returns that often pale in comparison to other investment avenues.

- **Cryptocurrencies**

Cryptocurrencies, virtual or digital currencies, pivot on cryptographic security. Their hallmark is high volatility, rendering them a high-risk domain.

- **Retirement Accounts**

Retirement accounts proffer tax incentives for long-term investment, and are devised to amass funds for retirement.

- **Peer-to-Peer Lending**

This avenue involves loaning money to individuals or businesses via online platforms, with returns reaped from interest on loan repayments.

- **Startups and Private Equity**

Venturing into startups and private companies implies extending capital in exchange for an ownership stake.

In the domain of investment, it's imperative to factor in your risk tolerance, investment horizon, and financial aspirations. Diversification, fanning out investments across varied asset classes, emerges as a pivotal strategy in risk management. Furthermore, remaining well-versed in market trends, economic landscapes, and the performance of your investments remains pivotal for judicious decision-making.

CHAPTER SEVEN

FINDING DIFFERENT WAYS TO GET PAID

Earning money is like a puzzle with many pieces. It's about getting money from different places like having a job, doing your own business, investing, or other ways to make money. This is a very important part of managing your money because it helps you pay for things you need every day, save up for big goals, and reach your financial dreams. Let's explore some common ways people earn money:

- **Employment Income**

Securing a job with a reliable salary or hourly wage is a common and straightforward way to earn money consistently. Consider industries that offer stability and potential for growth. Advancing your skills and seeking career development opportunities can lead to higher earning potential.

- **Self-Employment Income; Being Your Own Boss or Running a Business**

Starting a business can provide a regular income stream. Identify a viable business idea, create a business plan, and work towards building a customer base. While starting a business requires effort and investment, it can lead to financial independence and consistent earnings.

- **Money from Investments**

Earning money from investments means you put your money into things like stocks (owning parts of companies), bonds (lending money to governments or companies), or other things that can grow in value over time as discussed above.

Diversifying your investments can help create a balanced income portfolio.

- **Renting Out Properties**

Investing in real estate and renting out properties can lead to consistent rental income. Being a responsible landlord, maintaining properties, and cultivating positive tenant relationships are crucial for steady earnings in the long run. Imagine you have a house or apartment. You can earn money by letting others live there and paying you rent.

- **Getting Paid for Your Work**

If you write a book, compose music, or invent something, you can get paid when others want to use or buy your creation.

- **Earning Extra for Good Work**

Some people, especially in jobs like sales, earn more money when they do well. This can be a bonus on top of their regular pay.

- **Retirement Money**

When people retire, they can still get money from their old jobs or special accounts set up for retirement. These accounts give them money to live on when they're not working anymore.

- **Freelancing and consulting**

If you possess specialized skills, consider offering your services as a freelancer or consultant. Many businesses and individuals are willing to pay for services like writing, design, marketing, and consulting. Freelancing allows you to take on projects as they come and earn money on a per-project basis.

- **Part-Time Work**

Taking on part-time or temporary jobs in addition to your primary employment can supplement your income. Part-time roles provide flexibility and can help you explore different industries while earning extra money.

People who do part-time jobs, like driving for rideshare companies or doing tasks online, earn money based on the work they do.

- **Dividend-Paying Investments**

Investing in dividend-paying stocks, mutual funds, or exchange-traded funds (ETFs) can provide regular income through dividend payments. This strategy is especially attractive for long-term investors seeking steady returns.

- **Working Together with Others**

If you and others start a project or a business together, the money you make is based on how well things go and how much you own in the project.

- **Peer-to-Peer Lending**

Participating in peer-to-peer lending platforms allows you to lend money to individuals or businesses and earn interest on your loans. This strategy offers an alternative way to earn consistent returns.

- **Online Income Streams**

The digital landscape offers numerous opportunities for earning money. Blogging, affiliate marketing, e-commerce, and creating and selling digital products are avenues where you can generate regular income online. Building a loyal online audience or customer base is key to sustained earnings.

- **Subscription Services**

If you're a content creator, consider offering subscription-based services or products. This approach provides a predictable income stream as subscribers pay a regular fee to access your content or services.

- **Passive Income Streams**

Creating passive income involves setting up income streams that require minimal ongoing effort. Examples include royalties from books, music, or licensing your creative works. Building online courses, affiliate marketing, and earning through automated businesses are other ways to earn passively.

CHAPTER EIGHT

EMBRACING FINANCIAL FEMINISM LIFE

Living a financial feminist life means taking control of your financial destiny, championing equality, and embracing self-reliance in money management. It's about weaving feminist principles into your financial decisions and pursuits. Here's how to live a financial feminist life:

- Educate yourself about personal finance, investment strategies, and economic concepts. Armed with knowledge, you can make informed choices that align with your goals.

- Stand up for equal pay and opportunities in your career. Advocate for fair compensation, aim for promotions, and challenge gender-driven pay gaps.
- Forge Financial Independence. Strive for self-sufficiency by earning your own income and managing your financial affairs. Relying on yourself empowers you to shape your financial destiny.
- Invest in your future by setting aside funds for long-term goals like retirement, education, and

homeownership. Your financial stability matters.

- Approach debt cautiously. Focus on tackling high-interest debt and avoid being overwhelmed by financial obligations.
- Lift Women Entrepreneurs: Where feasible, support businesses run by women and female entrepreneurs. Your patronage fosters economic empowerment.
- Craft an emergency fund to cushion financial blows during tough times or unforeseen circumstances.
- Share Financial Wisdom: Promote financial literacy and empowerment among fellow

women and girls in your community. Elevate each other.

- Challenge conventional notions around gender and finance. Foster open financial discussions in relationships and partnerships.
- Advocate for financial services that cater to women's unique financial needs and situations.
- Develop negotiation skills and assertiveness in financial conversations, whether at work or in personal life.
- Drive Policy Change: Support policies that advance gender equality and economic justice.

CONCLUSION

A financial feminist embodies a woman who harnesses the influence of money not only for her benefit but also to uplift those around her. The primary objective is to equip women with the knowledge and tools required to master budgeting, savings, expenditure, salary negotiations, and investments – the essential components to navigate the intricacies of their financial journeys and achieve enduring stability.

This endeavor serves the purpose of delving into your financial concerns and identifying ways to bolster your fiscal groundwork. The time has come to translate insight into action and revolutionize your relationship with money. Devoting effort and time to educational resources becomes an investment in your financial prowess.

In doing so, women can actively participate in challenging the current financial framework that disproportionately disadvantages numerous women. By empowering themselves, they become agents of change in a system that demands reform

By following the steps discuss in the above chapters and being smart about your money, you can take charge of your finances, feel less worried, and work toward a better future. Just remember that money management is something you do all the time and little by little, it can make a big difference in your life.